Can I Have a Dinosaur?

Written by Virginia King   Illustrated by Mark Payne

"How would you like a dinosaur for a pet?" Miss Martin asked the class.

"My dad won't even let me have a pet dog," said Daniel. "He'd never let me have a dinosaur!"

"Well, why don't you ask him, just to be sure?" said Miss Martin.

The children looked at each other and then at Miss Martin. They all knew dinosaurs had been dead for millions of years.

Miss Martin explained. "If you use your imaginations, you can think what a pet dinosaur would be like," she said. "I want you to find out as much as you can about your favorite dinosaur, and then write your parents a letter, telling them why you would like it for a pet."

Daniel and the other children couldn't wait to get started. They spent a lot of time in the school library finding out exactly what their favorite dinosaurs looked like, where they liked to live, and what they ate.

Daniel's favorite was Tyrannosaurus Rex, and the next morning, as he was leaving for school, he handed his dad a letter.

They Ruled the EARTH
All ABOUT DINOSAURS
DINOSAURS

T. REX

Dear Dad,

I'm writing for a special reason. I think that I need a pet to look after — so that I can grow up to be responsible.

I would like a Tyrannosaurus Rex. Its ferocious teeth would make it very good at guarding the house. I could teach it to use its small front legs to beg for its supper. Please write back and say that I can have one.

Love from your son, *Daniel*

P.S. Have a good day at work.

Daniel was very excited that night when he found a letter on his pillow.

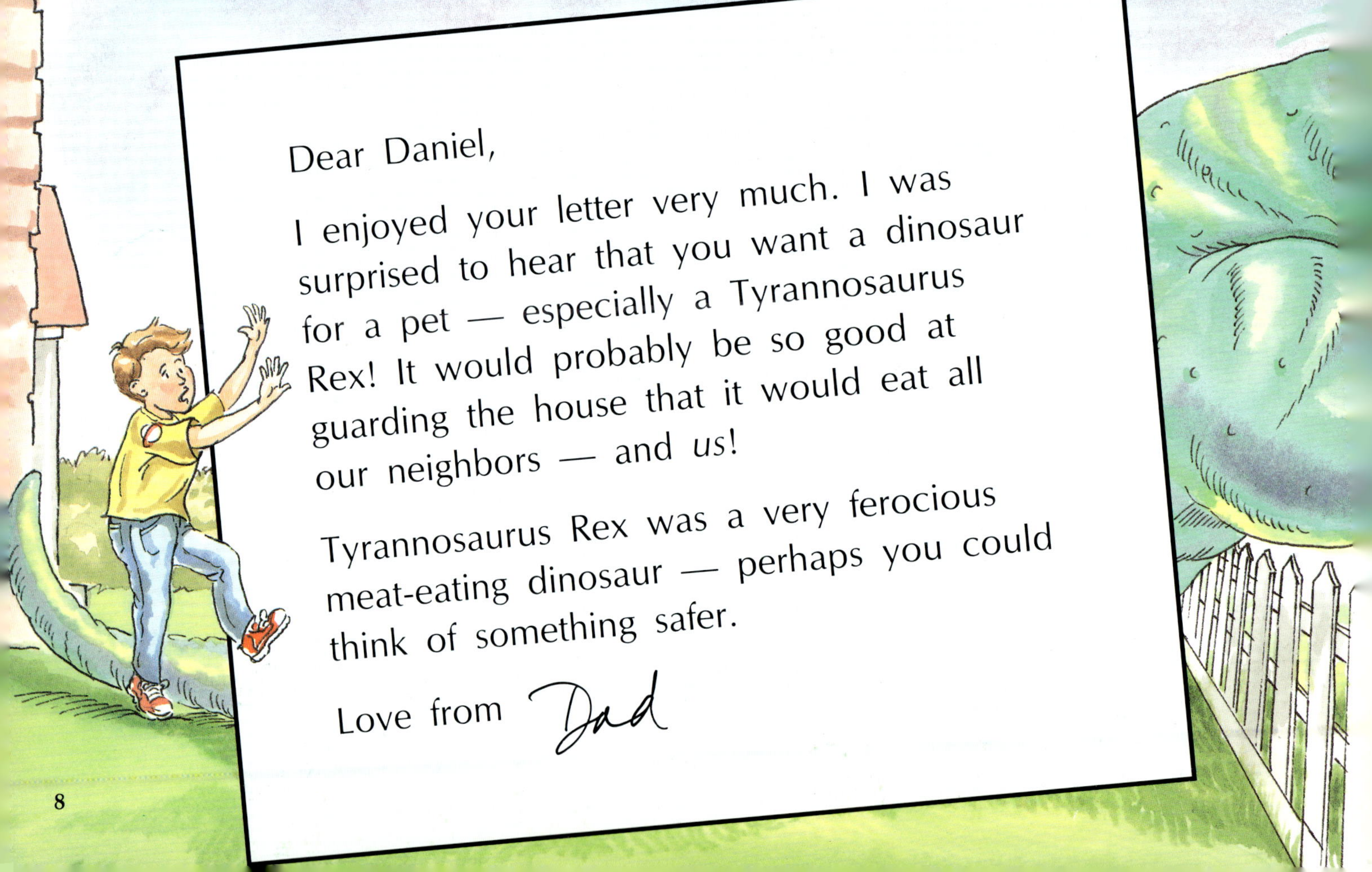

Dear Daniel,

I enjoyed your letter very much. I was surprised to hear that you want a dinosaur for a pet — especially a Tyrannosaurus Rex! It would probably be so good at guarding the house that it would eat all our neighbors — and *us*!

Tyrannosaurus Rex was a very ferocious meat-eating dinosaur — perhaps you could think of something safer.

Love from Dad

Dad

Daniel tried to remember all the different kinds of dinosaurs, to see if he could think of something safer than Tyrannosaurus Rex. The next morning he had an idea, and soon he and his dad were writing letters almost every day.

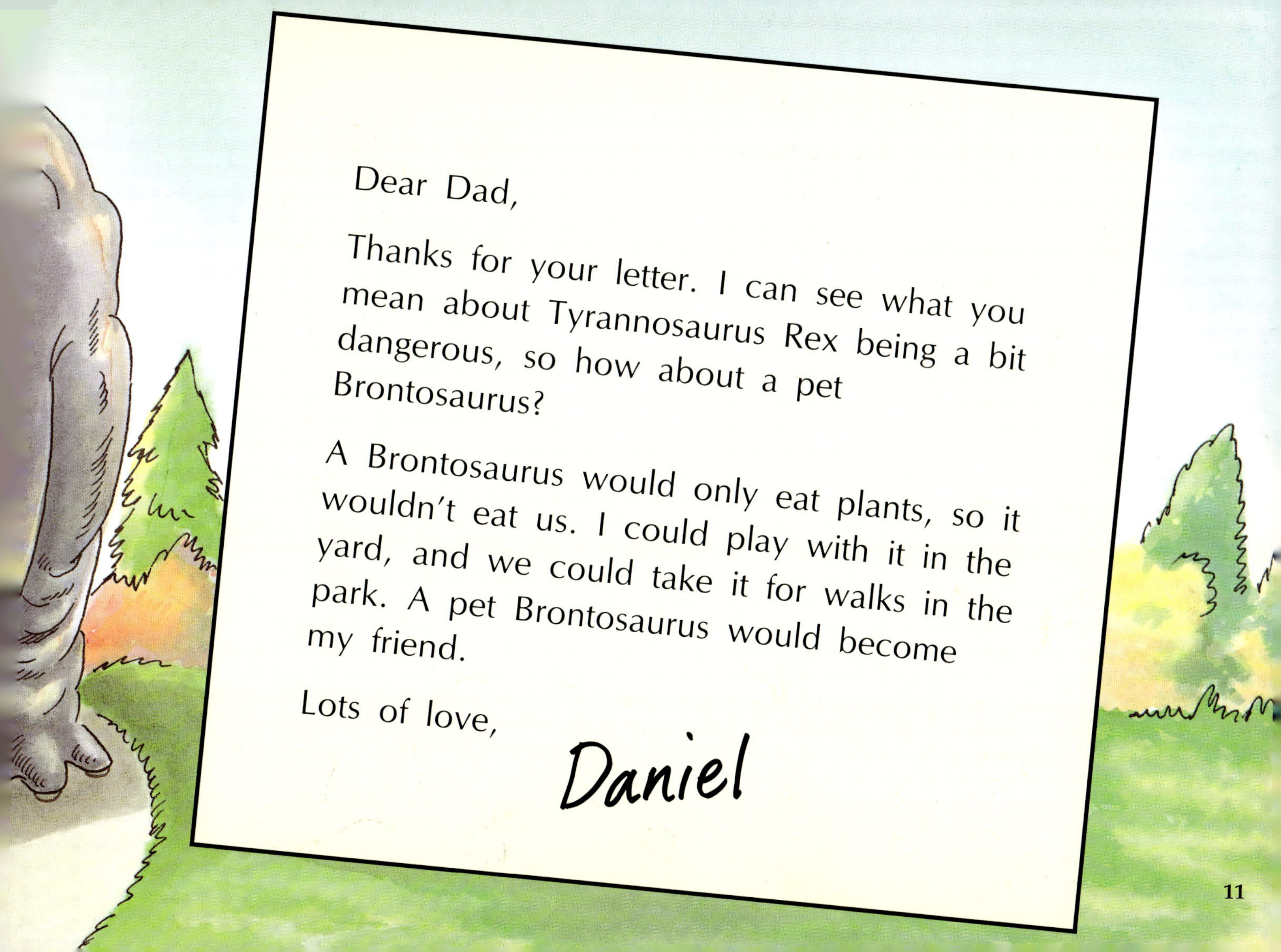

Dear Dad,

Thanks for your letter. I can see what you mean about Tyrannosaurus Rex being a bit dangerous, so how about a pet Brontosaurus?

A Brontosaurus would only eat plants, so it wouldn't eat us. I could play with it in the yard, and we could take it for walks in the park. A pet Brontosaurus would become my friend.

Lots of love,

Daniel

Dear Daniel,

Thank you for your letter about a Brontosaurus for a pet. It would certainly be much friendlier than a Tyrannosaurus Rex, but it would still be too big for our yard.

If you took it for a walk, its footsteps would make the whole neighborhood shake, and it would be so hungry that it would probably eat all the trees in the park! Perhaps you could think of a smaller pet.

Love from Dad

Dad
LUNCH

Dave

Dear Dad,

I think I've found the perfect dinosaur — Triceratops.

Triceratops is a smaller dinosaur than Brontosaurus. It wouldn't need a collar, because it's already got one! I could teach it to fetch a ball and bring in your newspaper. Its horns would make it a good guard dinosaur, too.

Love from

Daniel

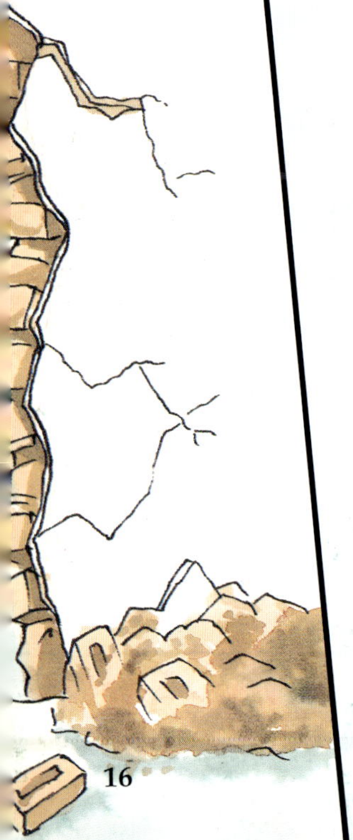

Dear Daniel,

A Triceratops is a much better choice, but I don't think you'd be able to teach it any tricks.

Dinosaurs had very small brains, so they probably didn't learn very quickly. Also, Triceratops had very short legs and was a very slow mover — not very good for chasing a ball. It might not be much fun to cuddle, either — all those sharp horns would get in the way. Why don't you think of a smoother pet?

Love from Dad

Dad

DAD

Dear Dad,

One of the Plesiosaurs would be a smooth pet. We could build a swimming pool for it to live in. We could feed it fresh fish, just like the seals at the zoo. It would be lots of fun to go swimming with — we could use its back as a slippery slide! And when it needed a bath we could just fill the pool with bubble bath. I think a Plesiosaur would make the best kind of pet of all the dinosaurs. I hope you agree.

Love from

Daniel

Dear Daniel,

I like your suggestion of a Plesiosaur for a pet. It would certainly be safe from everyone if it lived in a swimming pool. But have you thought about its sharp teeth — and where you would get enough fish to feed it? I also wonder whether it's really fair to keep a wild animal in such a small place. Do you think it would be happy?

Love from Dad

P.S. There's one big problem we haven't mentioned yet — dinosaurs are extinct!

Dear Dad,

You're right about dinosaurs not being perfect pets. But I still really want a pet to look after. What do you suggest?

Love from

Daniel

Dear Daniel,

I've been thinking a lot about the sort of pet that might be right for you. It seems to me that you want a pet that you can look after and take for walks in the park. You want a pet that can wear a collar, fetch a ball, bring in the paper, and guard the house. And you want a pet to play with — a pet that will become your friend.

Instead of a dinosaur for a pet, how about a dog?

Love from Dad

Dad

Can you guess what
Daniel wrote back?